Always Be Closing

Top Sales People's Training Techniques and strategies to Learn How to Perfect the Art of Selling to Anyone in Order to Get More Customers, Receive More Referrals and Earn More Money

By Omid Kazravan

Table of Contents

Your Gift

Because you took action to invest in yourself. I am giving you FREE access to a few bonuses

Go to www.Alwaysbempire.com NOW to get exclusive access to 6 different sales tracking worksheets that you can use and apply in your business TODAY! The best part about this offer is that it is completely free. No gimmicks.

TONY ROBBINS SAYS "What doesn't get measured doesn't get managed"

This is my gift to you to elevate your sales game.

Special Thanks go out to

Mom

Family

Juan

Nick

Luis

Find out the incredible impact that these individuals and several others have made in my life, in the

Thank You Section at the end of the book.

"Life is not a journey but a destination"

Introduction

Thank you all for joining me on this adventure and for tapping into your desire to take your life to the next level. If you're reading this book, not only are you committed to taking a new step in your life, but you're also halfway towards your journey to being a master closer.

Unfortunately, once we learn something we become comfortable with the skill and no longer pursue the learning process. Our comfort zone hinders us from developing even more.

My goal for this book is to change the way the sales game is viewed; it's not really about all of the closing techniques used when it comes to selling, but rather who you are as a person and how you sell yourself.

Did you know when it comes to purchasing a new vehicle it actually takes buyers more days to come to a decision now than it used to before? Why? Currently, consumers buy from people they TRUST. It comes down to the relationship built between the client(s) and the salesperson.

Additionally, it's not even about the product; it's about who we are as individuals and what we can provide to our client(s). What **value** are you really bringing to your client? Surely you had a situation in which you wanted to purchase something, but the sales professional was not only extremely assertive, but also made you feel uncomfortable. Even though you needed the product, you chose not to buy it due to the impudence received from the salesperson. This is what is happening in our industry right now. People are so focused on selling themselves to the customer they lose the sale.

I have this belief that we have been selling ourselves since birth. Every single interaction with every single person we have encountered has been has been a personal sales pitch. When you were a child whom wanted something from someone, you would convince the other person about how imperative it was for you to have the item, even stating you were willing to do anything for it. You were ultimately selling yourself and dependent on how well you sold yourself would determine whether or not you received the item.

In any job interview, you're selling yourself to the interviewer or to the company. Being hired equates to him/her/it "buying you."Often the people hired are the ones more liked rather than more qualified.

Are you beginning to see a pattern right now? For those of you that have been in a relationship or are currently in one, let me explain how it works. When you're progressing towards something more than friends, you are basically letting your partner know what you can bring to the table or who you really are. When a relationship begins, your partner has chose to "purchase" your product, you. Furthermore, for those in a long-term relationship, you were "selling yourself" on a day-to-day basis resulting in your partner choosing to "purchase" you every single day. Each human interface is always a sales interaction. You will always be closing because you will continually be selling yourself.

In this book the beginning will set the framework for becoming an expert at selling yourself. It will create the foundation on how to continuously close. As stated, it's not all about the techniques for the doing; being is also a huge part.

If I said to you, "Hey, let's go build a mansion" and I continued with, "on sand," would you agree? If your answer is yes, I'm very glad you purchased this book because building a house on an unstable foundation will lead to a great deal of problems. Since it's a shaky foundation it will constantly shift and move, making it unstable and not a good platform for growth.

What we are doing in sales is "building a home on a solid foundation." In this book, I am asking you to build a home with me, not on sand, but on a solid, concrete foundation. Each chapter segways into the next to allow you to absorb all of the information easily.

I want to make one last thing clear as we begin our journey together. Just because someone signs up for a gym membership does not mean they will be in shape, the same can be said about this book—just because you purchased it does not mean you will be successful in sales. You must make a commitment prior to beginning this book to read it from cover to cover and then apply what you learn. This book will open the doors for you and show you the path; I cannot push you through the door, just like you cannot hire someone to do your own push-ups. It is something that you must do yourself. There is no such thing as an elevator for success, you must be willing to take the stairs and put in the work required for your success.

At the end of every single chapter I have left you some space where you can write your final thoughts on each chapter in order to take them in even more. I have placed a "*sign here*" for you to make a commitment to yourself to use anything you find valuable in this book.

X

I'm very excited to teach you everything I know about being a master on how to sell yourself!

"There's nothing more dangerous than a closed mind."

Chapter 1: A major shift

If you made the decision to read this book, then you already have an open mind and will be receptive to learning new things to improve your performance as a salesperson. Often, our egos interfere with our learning new, beneficial things; we believe we already know the information or we convince ourselves the information will not work for us since we know everything about our field and nothing will improve our skillset.

As a leader in sales, I am asking you not to read this book with your ego, but instead open your mind for the possibilities that await. At the conclusion of the book, you will have tidbits to help you skyrocket your sales and assist you in producing your goal numbers.

There is a speaker who shares a story of attending a seminar with Tony Robbins, a famous motivational speaker. At the seminar, Tony was feverishly writing notes while the other speaker looked at him questioning how he could write so much. At the end of the day, the two speakers were comparing their notes; Tony's notebook was filled from cover to cover while the other speaker only has a couple of pages in his book. In absolute shock, he asked Tony how and why he did it. Tony responded by stating whenever in a learning environment he attends as if he knows absolutely nothing about the topic to allow all of the information to flow without a filter in his mind so he can capture that one golden nugget.

Our first chapter is going to be about the mindset shift that we need to make. There are things we need to unlearn in order to learn new things. This is the reason why many companies, especially car dealerships, love to hire new salesman, as to not be burdened with some bad habits that accompany older salespeople.

This is not to say you have bad habits, but tackling the things you learned in the beginning of your training to build a solid foundation need to be changed, or at least altered.

You can't sell to everyone

A mistake made by many sales people is trying to sell every single person walking in. What happens when you try to sell to everyone is people can sniff out your intentions very easily. You will come off as needy and brash or from a place of scarcity, which is not a good thing. It's like dating; just because you find someone attractive does not mean you will date.

It is important to be open to whatever comes your way. When we have an intention to sell to every single person, we are more committed to the sale than to the person.

Sales are all about the other person. Instead of focusing on selling to every single person, focus on **serving** every single person. When you shift from selling to the person to serving the person, it will make a difference in your business and your career.

It's this one mindset shift of serving everyone that walks through your doors that you need to adopt. When you are focused on serving, you tend to treat people differently because you are attentive to them and not yourself. Typically, when we focus on ourselves, others can sense our insincerity

A very easy way to achieve the focus and attention on our customer is through questioning ourselves because where focus goes, energy flows.

Questions to ask yourself:

- *How can I serve this person right now?*
- *How can I be more present in this moment?*
- *What does this person need?*

Once you have this mindset shift, the game will change for you. If you consider if you wanted to purchase something, would you want to be treated as a dollar sign or as a person? You would be more willing to work with and purchase a product or service from a salesperson that makes you feel important rather than another sale or number.

This is exactly how I become one of the top salesmen in my company. I worked at a dealership and knew absolutely nothing about cars or any tricks on how to sell them. The majority of my coworkers were 10-30 years older me and had multiple years of professional sales experience under their belts. However, even though they had been in the industry longer than I, it didn't deter me.

I knew what I wanted, why I wanted it, and how to treat people. I understood the concept that people do not care how much you know until they know how much you care. Due to the way I treated my customers, I received a multitude of referrals that would allow me to close about 75% of every sale with each person I spoke to.

What does the statement, "People don't care how much you know until they know how much you care"? Think back to a time when there was not a hidden intention, only the concept of making the other person happy. If you take one important thing from this book, it should be this concept; this idea of serving your customer will get you to where you need to be and set you apart from the other salespeople.

I was so confident in the way I treated people I would ask to work with a coworker's customer when he or she would lose a sale; since I treated the customer like royalty, it would result in a sale for me. I even had instances in which the customer liked me so much he or she tipped me extra money, as if I was a waiter. As a result, my coworkers would question what I was doing, but I would just smile as I high-fived the family I just sold to. I've had customers invite me to their family dinners, to go out on the town with them, and others who have returned with gifts simply because of how I treated them.

The Golden Rule states to treat others how you want to be treated. But there is a rule above that, which is even greater! Start with the concept of treating people the way you want to be treated; by putting yourself first, you usually treat others with a ton of respect because that's how you want to be treated. The only flaw in this rule is again the focus is on you. This is why there is a higher rule—the Platinum Rule.

The Platinum Rule is to treat others the way *they* want to be treated. It doesn't matter how you want to be treated or what you think is correct in your model of the world. It all depends on the person you are serving in your sale.

Think about it, if someone comes in to purchase something and you treat him or her EXACTLY how he or she wants to be treated, even if he or she doesn't make a purchase, he or she will remember you and possibly refer you to other people.

The following chapters will discuss how to identify how people want to be treated and how to get them to elicit their needs to you so you don't have to do any of the work. You never want to *make* your customer buy; you want to *let* them buy. By being a steward of service and guiding your customer through the sales process, he or she will eventually want to make the purchase.

Write down your major takeaways!

_____

"when you feel like quitting think about why you started"

Chapter 2: Compelling Reason WHY

When you order a burger, whether a cheeseburger or a veggie burger, the most important part of a burger is the patty. I don't think I've ever enjoyed a burger that lacked a patty and I think it's safe to assume you probably haven't either.

In this chapter, we will discuss the "patty of life," especially when it comes to sales—your reason WHY. This is essentially what everything comes down to since without it there is no flavor, no drive, or no higher purpose to keep you going with your sales.

If your sales rely on daily selling, I know the feeling when an entire day goes by without a single sale; it is one of the worst feelings. Spending 13 hours at my dealership, speaking to a ton of people, and yet not selling to one person. From all of the salespeople I have spoken to, this is what could make or break your whole month, unless you become more empowered.

You may be asking how this will help to always be top in sales upon closing. It is simply because sales does not only come down to one area of your life; your sales and the way you treat people comes down to *every* area of your life and how you show up. Your reason WHY you want to be in sales, and be the best, is how you will be a top salesperson.

When a moment approaches in which you're facing defeat face-to-face, it's your reason WHY that will help you win the battle and come out victorious. Your WHY will give you energy to keep going, help you hold your position at the top, or even pass the top salesperson and claim that position for yourself.

I knew exactly what my WHY was — I really wanted to be a salesman like one of my mentors. After about 10 months of shuttling with the person in charge of running the sales department, I kept hitting roadblocks. He kept rejecting me over and over again. Then he told me to get a sales job, rise to the top, and return to him in 6 months. Thus that's exactly what I did; I got hired at my dealership and immediately started to climb the leader board.

My WHY was getting my dream job at the time. I was not going to allow anything to get in my way. Anytime I would get tired or unmotivated, I would just ask myself WHY did I start this journey? Once I was able to reassure myself of my reasons, nothing could stop me.

This is what will propel you forward into your greatness.

Your WHY is the patty of your life; it's where you draw your inspiration and your motivation to do something. It's where you find out why something is causing you pain as well as why something is bringing you pleasure. Your WHY allows you to decode anything in your life and recode it. WHY allows you to reverse engineer anything you want and is the single greatest tool you need in your tool belt of life when it comes to creating something.

You may be wondering; how do I find **my** WHY? There is a simple process to help you find it.

First, start off by asking yourself these questions:

- *What am I excited for in life?*
- *Who do I need to be in order to be the best salesperson I could be?*
- *What do I want to accomplish with my sales?*
- *Why do I want to accomplish these goals?*

Once you have found the answers for each of these questions, start questioning your own answer.

For example:

- What am I excited for in life?: I am excited for the opportunity to be able to tell my mother she never has to work a day in her life again. I'm excited to share my message with people around the world and to impact those who need it.

- Why do I want to do all of this? I want to do this because my mother is the reason I am where I am today and she deserves to enjoy her life now. When I was younger, someone shared his message with me and it changed my life. If I were to quit now, then others would not hear my message and it might change the path of their life.

Do you see how I basically decoded the already decoded answer? The reason we need to delve deeper is the reason why this tool is so powerful. Whenever you look at all the great people of the world — the Mozarts or Jordans or Shakespeares—the reason they're where they are (or were) is because of their WHY; it propels them to be more empowered and exceptional.

Take a look at the top sales professional in your field; there's a reason he or she is producing on a day-to-day basis. In my dealership there was one older man that would outsell everyone every single month. Unfortunately, this man was also the most dishonest in the dealership and would constantly receive bad reviews. However, his work ethic was off the charts, working 7 days a week and13 hours a day. When people would finish the month with 35 sales, he would end with 44. Unfortunately, everyone would snicker behind his back and complain that he would always come out on top, but no one asked him how or why he did it. One day I took the liberty of sharing lunch with him and he explained he had 3 kids in college and wanted to make sure they would not have a problem living the life they wanted to live; he wanted to be the one to provide for them before he passed. He also jokingly said his wife doesn't like when he's home so he comes to work so he can also make her happy.

Do you see how powerful his WHY was? It pushed him every single day to work to make all of those sales to earn commission for his family to be better off than he was.

Once you start to decode your answers and start to understand why you want each thing, you might come across a pattern of commonalities. This is where you grab everything that excites you about WHY you're doing what you want to do and create your ultimate WHY.

Remember, your WHY is for YOU; what other people think about your WHY is irrelevant because it's your life. Typically what I've found is, that people that set their WHYs to something outside of themselves or greater than themselves are more compelled to accomplish their goals because they are not as focused on themselves. However, if focusing on yourself is what works for you, then go for it.

Also keep in mind this WHY does not have to stay with you your whole life; as you mature and improve your way of life each day, your WHY will alter as well. You will not be the same person today as you will be in five years, thus, it's okay if your WHY alters along the way as you're beliefs, values, and rules change. Don't think you're taking this WHY to the grave with you; once you detach from that and allow it to serve you in the present moment then you'll allow your WHY to serve your needs much easier.

Consistency

Have you ever witnessed how some people are always consistent with what they've set out to do? Regardless of what obstacle comes their way, they still find a way to achieve their goals. The only reason they do is because they have a strong enough WHY propelling them through the tough times.

Tough times will come for everyone. Life will throw curve balls at you, but if you have your WHY ready to stand up against the tough times and impose its stance, you, too, can battle the tough times head-on and be victorious.

Fitness has always been a catalyst in my life; I am extremely grateful for my journey because if not for it I would not be where I am today. I have spent a multitude of years learning about fitness, but, admittedly, I have also spent those years stopping and going in my fitness lifestyle. I was a fitness dabbler; there were times when I would start and set huge goals for myself and then a few months later I would become too comfortable and it would fade away until I would stop working out completely. Of course, several months later I would start back up again. It was a cycle, but it was a cycle that thrust me forward in my journey.

No matter how hard I worked out or I disliked my body or I educated myself, I would keep finding excuses to stop. I was never compelled enough to finish. I had no vision, no purpose behind it — it was meaningless.

When something is meaningless, we tend to pay less attention to it because we do not see any value coming from it. As much as I wanted that change, as much as I would restart and change my approach, I would keep getting the same results until I changed that one factor.

I needed my vision — my WHY — so I could keep going. Consistency comes from having a clear vision of where you're going. If you do what you've always done, you'll continue to have the same results. An imperative part of the success cycle is to change your approach when something is not working in order to tackle the challenge again. Unless you change the root problem, your cycle will continue.

An alarming point is when you believe a problem in one area of your life will only remain in that specific area. Be that as it may, issues are not usually a surface level problem, but rather a deeper-seeded consequence that needs to be resolved. In my case, it was not having a clear and defined purpose. Not only was it showing up in my health regimen, but it was also showing up in other areas of my life as well.

When times become tough, your best action is not reaction, but to take a step back from the situation. Either sit or lay down, go to a quiet space, or whatever you feel more comfortable doing and place your hand over your heart; begin to breathe deeply and feel your heart beating. By clearing your mind and focusing on the beating of your heart, it allows you to be grateful for your heart and for its beating automatically for you. As you are sitting there breathing life into your heart and filling your mind with gratitude, start to ask yourself WHY. Visualize your why coming to life: start to imagine the feelings running through your body when it happens. Feel what you would feel when it's done, see what you would see when it's accomplished, hear what you would hear when you finally reach it, and allow your whole being to experience the power of your WHY.

This is how you reconnect and allow your WHY to continue to empower you. It's a heart-breathing meditation that allows you to refocus and re-center yourself when your life starts to feel the shockwaves from the earthquake known as your life.

Allow this clear image of your future to be your paintbrush to color your new blank canvas you have created and use this power to extend your sales.

Write down your major takeaways!

"People don't care how much you know, until they know how much you care"

Chapter 3: Silver tongue

Have you ever been in a conversation in which you were "speaking" with someone and other person monopolizes the conversation yet claims he/she really enjoyed the conversation? Even though you didn't say one single word?

The reason for this is people love to talk about themselves, especially when it's someone that will offer all of their attention and just listen without interrupting or judging. This is such an essential skill to have in life, especially when it comes to ABC.

As previously stated, people don't care how much you know until they know how much you care. Don't be that salesperson that just rambles on about your life or about your product with no intention or purpose.

The first thing I do when a customer walks into my dealership is greet him or her by asking his or her name and what is the purpose of their visit. I listen intently to his or her exact words; once I know why he or she is in my showroom, I discuss how to find a car on our computer website. This is the part in which I take over the conversation because I explain how our company works and how the process of selecting a car works.

If a customer disagrees with me during this period, I do not argue back, but rather allow them to finish speaking, agree with him or her, then change the direction of the topic to something more empowering to serve both of us. You never want to disagree with your customer because it immediately destroys the rapport you have built.

After changing the subject, I escort my customer to the vehicles and allow him or her to explore everything alone. Hovering can be intimidating and bothersome and possibly lose the sale. I inform my customer where I will be if he or she needs me and I will help. The madness behind this tactic is to allow the customer to sell to him/herself since he or she knows exactly what he/she wants and I was not going to make him or her fall in love with a car he or she was not looking for just because I would get a higher commission. I want to serve my customer and his/her needs.

When we converse, it is always focused on the customer. If I am asked a question, I briefly answer the question and then switch the focus back to the customer. The key to conversing with a customer is to keep the discussion at a 80/20 medium in which you're listening 80% of the time and only talking 20% of the time. Sometimes the best form of communication is to listen. Keeping it at a80/20 range will grant the customer the ability to trust you as well.

The way to keep the conversation flowing with a customer is to ask open-ended questions that do not lead to a simple yes or no answer and can be branched off into another topic. For example, "How did you end up in this area?" allows you to learn a little about your customer's history, which opens up more paths when it comes to asking other questions. By delving into the customer's lifestyle, you are able to assist more in the sale. For example, if a woman comes in and states her children are all in college, you do not want to suggest a minivan because it will not fit her lifestyle and she may leave without making a sale; however, if you suggest she does something for herself and show her the new sports car, she may suggest you to her friends whom are in the same position in life — and now your sales may double or triple.

Another thing I want to make clear is questioning is part of being a salesperson whom services his/her customers. You must actually be interested in what your customer has to say because you're not asking a multitude of questions just to close a sale, but because you actually care and you're actually interested in what your customer has to say.

This is how you become a very affable person whom your customers enjoy being around and feel comfortable placing their trust in.

Rapport

For those of you who are unaware, rapport is a harmonious relationship you form with another. It is a form of neurolinguistic programming (NLP), or the three elements (neurology, language, and programming) that encompass the human experience. Rapport used on a daily basis to forge a feeling of trust and understanding. An easier way to understand this in a situation when you meet someone for the first time yet you feel like you've known him or her for a long time because your personalities mesh so well.

Basically, rapport makes it very easy to close on a sale with the customer because he/she will trust and understand you. It's the art of being in harmony with your customer to make him/her feel so GOOD about he or she will want to be around you.

Rapport is a skill you need to add into your communication tool belt. There are various books on this topic so feel free to continue your studying if you want to learn more. I am a huge advocate of constant and never-ending improvement.

Building Rapport

To build rapport, we:

- Smile
- Matching and mirroring
- Find common ground
- Speak their language
- Build on their ideas
- Be honest
- Pace & lead

Remember, you're not selling; you're making a friend. You want to make it familiar for the customer. People like others they can find a similarity with and can relate to. If you follow the steps to build rapport, you and your customer will have a harmonious relationship, which can only lead to a sale.

The first step is to Smile.

Smiling is so important, yet we don't do enough of it. I remember one day looking around my showroom during peak hours and during slow hours and everyone was taciturn and carried stress and disappointment on their face. NO! Don't do this! Smiling is such a powerful tool when it comes to sales because it makes you trustworthy and it makes you extremely approachable. When you smile it shows you're happy and enjoying yourself and people want to be around someone who is giving off such positive energy. By no means am I saying to have a huge creepy, clown smile glued to your face, but a nice, genuine, and inviting smile will turn your whole day around.

I remember one of my new coworkers absolutely increasing his volume the first month selling. I asked him how he was doing it yet I automatically knew the answer; I wanted to be around this person all the time, especially because his smile warmed the room. When he was working with one customer, others would patiently and happily wait for him to finish all his tasks because he had such a powerful and positive energy about him.

The next step is Matching and Mirroring.

This is another way of building rapport using body language. Matching and mirroring is one of the simplest, yet effective, ways of building rapport because it allows you to be like the other person. To do this, subtly match and mirror what the other person is doing with his or her body during the conversation. For example, if you see your customer reach out and scratch his head, reach out and scratch your head as well. If you see your customer take a sip of water, take a sip of water as well. If he sits a certain way, you sit that same exact way.

Again, remember we are building trust and likability with the customer. You must perfect the art of matching and mirroring in an elusive way and you'll realize the person will begin to respond to you even more.

Step three is to Find Common Ground.

Finding common ground is building rapport through communication by finding something you have in common with your client. Whether it is the movies you like or maybe even a hobby, there is always something you can share with a person to build rapport.

You need to probe your client by asking questions so you can immediately find a commonality to build on. Remember, people flock to those like them.

Let me share an example of excellent rapport skills. My aunt was a door-to-door saleswoman for Tony Robbins; she would go into a business and ask to speak to a manager in order to book a presentation and sell tickets for one of Mr. Robbins' events. After smooth talking the front desk people, she eventually was sitting in front of the general manager of the dealership. Unfortunately, he was not giving her any of his attention because he was working and did not care what she had to say because he was extremely closed-minded. As she sat in the office trying to get his attention to discuss her proposal, he was not even making eye contact with her and giving her extremely dry answers as she was trying to close a deal. That is until she saw his phone light up with a screensaver of him and a Lamborghini. Immediately, she knew she had something to use to find common ground. She said to him, "Oh that's such a nice car! It's one of my favorites. Is it yours?" At that moment, the manager was hooked, paused what he was doing, focused on her, and proceeded to talk about the car for hours while my aunt just listened. Can you guess what happened next? She spoke to the entire business and sold her tickets all because of the rapport she established with the manager.

Next, you must learn to Speak their Language.

This is where your listening skills will be tested. By speaking your customer's language, he/she will begin to respond to you. Rapport is a harmony between people and that's what you want to create. Listen to the way your customer speaks; Does he use his body a lot? Is she loud?

Does he repeat a certain phrase multiple times? Does she describe things through sounds, feelings, or visuals?

There are5 categories people identify with:

- ✓ Visual
- ✓ Audio
- ✓ Kinesthetic (movement)
- ✓ Olfactory (smell)
- ✓ Gustatory (taste)

As you can see, all of these relate to our five senses.

Once you find out which one pertains to your customer the most, you can begin to "speak" his or her language.

You need to learn to distinguish the words they use to describe their experiences. People tend to repeat words that resemble them the most. It is up to you when you're communicating to listen intently to them and use the word(s) that resonates with them. Again it makes you a much more congenial person because you're speaking on the same level.

For anyone bilingual reading this book, I know when you meet someone in public that speaks the same foreign language as you, there is an immediate relationship and bond forged just because of your language! Thus, as a salesperson listen to your client's language pattern and reciprocate it.

Build on their Ideas.

As you can see, we're making a full circle to make the customer feel GOOD. You cannot be the significant one when it comes to sales because it will get in the way of your service and will be hard for you to reach the client. If your customer recommends something, BUILD ON IT! Encourage it, thank him/her for the idea, and give compliments on it. If you say something and he/she repeats it, celebrate and award him or her and recommend something that will add to it. Build the client's ego, not yours.

Be Honest.

Be a clear, transparent piece of paper when speaking to clients so everything is out on the table and you are not hiding anything. Honesty is the easiest way to maintain rapport because dishonesty is the fastest way to lose trust and a relationship with someone in a heartbeat. Make sure you have a level of honesty about you that can easily be seen and is comforting to others.

Many people have negative associations with anyone working in sales so they're afraid to work with us. Someone has either misrepresented them or they have heard horror stories from others. This is why they are guarded when they enter our showrooms. That's where you come in to save the day because you're not in it for the dollar, but rather because you actually care for them. Once their guard goes down, there's nothing but pure honesty on both ends.

The final step is Pacing and Leading.

How do you know when you finally have rapport with someone? As I mentioned earlier, rapport is like harmony, a dance of trust between two or more people. This is where pacing and leading come into the situation to help you gauge if you have a rapport with the other person. For example, start to pace yourself by following their lead such as if someone speaks extremely low, you start speak in a low pitch as well.

Once you have spent enough time using all of these techniques to build rapport with your client it's time to test it by leading them through something. For example, if you have a good rapport with someone and you began to raise your speaking volume, his or her volume will increase as well because you both are in harmony. Now you're in control of the situation and have a level of rapport that is based on trust and understanding. This is the ultimate form of communication.

One of my sales managers put it the best when he told me, "Omid, what you're doing when you're serving the customer is exactly like a bank transaction. You're constantly depositing into the account and once you have deposited enough, you can begin to withdraw when it comes time to ask for the sale." You have to make deposits in order to make withdrawals for if you have no money in the bank and try to make a withdrawal the ATM will reject you. However, if you're constantly making deposits, you will always be able to go back to the bank to retrieve money.

Customers are one and the same; you have to earn the right to make a withdrawal by constantly making deposits in the form of outstanding customer service, answering questions, and guidance in the buying experience. When it's time to ask for the NOW commitment, YOU HAVE EARNED THE RIGHT TO MAKE THAT WITHDRAW.

The longer you serve the customer and you treat them how they want to be treated, the more you're depositing into your savings account with your customer.

Write down your major takeaways!

"Relationships are the true currency of life."

BONUS CHAPTER

Remember Names = Stronger Connections = More Sales

As you have already learned about, when it comes to closing the sale, nothing can be more important than having a strong connection with the potential customer. In "How to Win Friends and Influence People," Dale Carnegie says that the sweetest sound to a person's ear is when they hear their name. Successfully recalling the name of someone you are trying to do business with, can make that transition from potential to actual client happen much more easily.

My Memory Coach, Memory Master Champion on Superhuman, and Best-Selling Author of "How to Remember Names and Faces," Luis Angel, taught me how to make it easier for me to memorize and learn the names of everyone that I meet.

I remember this one customer that I was on the verge of selling a vehicle to until something came up on his side. He came in to the dealership, I shook his hand, and we exchanged names. I said, "Hi how's it going, my name is Omid, what's your name?" He said, "My name is, Jeff but my friends call me Trump." I immediately used the techniques that Luis taught me and visualized Jeff with Donald Trump's fluffy hair. After I took him through the entire sales process we got to the point where Trump was going to hand over his down payment, when he told me that he couldn't do it. He said he had some sort of family emergency he had to handle. So he stood up, thanked us for our time and walked out.

A month after this took place, I saw him walk in the dealership. I threw my hands in the air and yelled "TRUMPPPPPPPPPP, WHATSUP!!!" He looked at me extremely surprised and said "YOOOOOOOOO!!! I CANT BELIEVE YOU REMEMBERED ME! I brought my wife here and we're both ready to buy cars and I can't wait to work with you again!" Trump told me that he's never become such good friends with a salesman before. Now, instead of only selling him one car, Trump ended up purchasing 2 vehicles. The memory technique helped me make this possible.

I have partnered up with Luis Angel to take a few examples from his book, which you can get at www.RememberNamesBook.com, and help you to start developing this skill of remember anyone's name and face.

He says that the Key to Memorization is Visualization. To turn anything that you want to memorize or remember, into a visual story.

So with names, all you have to do is take the name, turn it into a picture, and associate that image on the person's face.

The AE Mind Memory System by Luis Angel

1. Location: What Stands Out About This Individual?

2. Visualize: What Does This Name Remind Me of? Store the picture on the location.

3. Review: What did I picture on this individual's location?

Take a look at Name Game #1 to get some examples as to how this works.

NAME GAME: 1

Let's go ahead and practice right now with 12 names. I'll give you my picture representation for each one of these names:

Name = Picture

1. Abby = A Bee
2. Al = Owl
3. Angel = Angel Wings
4. Ann = Ant
5. Bridget = Bridge
6. Fred = Fred Flintstone
7. James = Chains
8. Luis = Lace (shoe)
9. Peggy = Pegged Leg
10. Rosa = Red Rose
11. Teddy = Teddy Bear
12. Wanda = Wand

Now those are my picture representations for the names. If one of them doesn't quite resonate with you or you feel that you can come up with a better image, by all means feel free to do that.

Let's go ahead and put this to the test. How about we take those names from up above and attach them to some faces?

I have both the Name of the Person and the Picture for that Name right underneath the Face.

Choose some facial features that stand out about that individual, and then take the image for the name and visualize it doing something on that location.

Al (*Owl*)	Luis (*Lace*)	Bridget (*Bridge*)
Fred (*Flinstone*)	Peggy (*Pegged Leg*)	James (*Chains*)
Abby (*A Bee*)	Teddy (*Bear*)	Wanda (*Wand*)
Angel (*Wings*)	Ann (*Ant*)	Rosa (*Red Rose*)

Great! Now that you have all 12 down, let's see
how many of those you can recall.

Don't worry about spelling. If you write down
Anne instead of Ann, it is perfectly fine.

ANSWERS FOR NG: 1

1. Al

2. Luis

3. Bridget

4. Fred

5. Peggy

6. James

7. Abby

8. Teddy

9. Wanda

10. Angel

11. Ann

12. Rosa

How did you do?

Did you get all of them correct? Most of them?

If you missed any, ask yourself "Why?"

Why do you think that you missed that name? Was the visual association not strong enough? Maybe you didn't resonate too well with the image representation that I have for that name. If that's the case, make sure to choose a picture representation for that name that you like.

If you got them all right, congratulations!

You were probably saying, "This was easy!" That could possibly be the case. I gave you some pretty easy names to memorize. You could quickly translate those names into images. Abby is A Bee. Al is an Owl. Those are pretty easy to see.

Now you're probably asking, "What about more complex names like Rebecca or Alexander?" It's the same process. Rebecca is a Rowing Book. Alexander is a Leg Sander. You take the name and ask yourself, "What does this name remind me of?"

NAME GAME: 2

The next 12 names and pictures for those names are as follows:

Name = Picture

1. Brad = Bread

2. Brent = Bran Cereal

3. Cannon = Cannon

4. Felix = Felix the Cat

5. Harper = Harp

6. Mary = Wedding Veil

7. Mike = Microphone

8. Nicole = Nickel

9. Pearl = White Pearl

10. Ron = Man Running

11. Ruth = Babe Ruth Chocolate

12. Tracy = Tracing with Pencil

Tracy	Harper	Ruth
Ron	Brent	Felix
Cannon	Mike	Mary
Nicole	Pearl	Brad

ANSWERS FOR NG: 2

1. Tracy

2. Harper

3. Ruth

4. Ron

5. Brent

6. Felix

7. Cannon

8. Mike

9. Mary

10. Nicole

11. Pearl

12. Brad

How did you do?

Did you get them all right?

Remember to make the visual association very strong and vivid. It will get easier the more that you do this.

NAME GAME: 3

Here's another go at it with 12 new names with their pictures:

Name = *Picture*

1. Ashley = Ashes
2. Ben = Bench
3. Billie = Billy Goat
4. Claudia = Cloud
5. Jo = Sloppy Jo
6. Jose = Water Hose
7. Leon = Lion
8. Oliver = Olive
9. Paige = Page (paper)
10. Pat = Pat with Hand
11. Phil = Gas Pump
12. Rex = T-Rex

Phil

Jo

Ben

Ashley

Oliver

Paige

Rex

Leon

Claudia

Billie

Jose

Pat

1. Phil

2. Jo

3. Ben

4. Ashley

5. Oliver

6. Paige

7. Rex

8. Leon

9. Claudia

10. Billie

11. Jose

12. Pat

How did you do here?

I hope that you are getting the hang of it!

In his Remember Names Book, Luis has over 500 of these examples for you to continue to practice with in order to become a master of names. Be sure to get your copy today at:

www.RememberNamesBook.com

Chapter 4: Spider Webbing

Imagine a web filled with an unlimited amount of connections and possibilities. This web is the network of every single person you have interacted with, where you reap what you sow This is where it's okay when you don't end up selling to every single person because if you don't make the sale with that person there are about 200 people in their network that you also gained access to if you won over their trust.

I remember the time I moved to Orlando, Florida after getting a new job at a local car dealership and I was getting myself settled into my new apartment. The only challenge was it was an unfurnished apartment and I needed to buy furniture. Since I was working all of the time, I immediately went shopping on my first day off. I heard some great reviews about a furniture warehouse so I decided to stop in there first. As soon as I arrived, I was greeted by a salesman who seemed to be seasoned as he answered a few of my questions and showed me towards the furniture I was looking for. I remember looking at some furniture and through my peripheral vision I saw the salesman slowly monitoring what I was doing. He then came back to me and tried to push a sale in my face without building any rapport or treating me like a person. I could easily tell I was a dollar sign for him and

I brushed him off and told him I was just looking, though I was ready to buy at that moment. I walked around more looking at other pieces and he approached me again, forcing me from where I was interested and pushing the original sale on me. Eventually he tried to give me an "irresistible offer," but it progressed to a point in which I felt like I was being choked by this "salesman" and I left without making a purchase.

Don't be like this salesman who not only lost the sale, but he has also lost my network. I remember over the course of my time in Orlando I would mention this man to friends every now and again when I would share my story about purchasing furniture. I'm sure it was a great company, but the way he represented it pushed me away and I never ended up buying from them nor did I recommend it.

I'm now mentioning this story because when I think of a poor salesman; he is the one I immediately remember. He lost a lot of potential customers just because he pushed me away and tried to sell me instead of serve me.

It's unfortunate, but I know everyone reading this book has encountered something like this; however, as a salesperson, you must understand you're not dealing with one person, you're dealing with an entire network of people—friends, family, and new acquaintances that will come their way.

This is why I'm stressing to treat your customers exactly how they want to be treated so you can tap into their whole network. When someone purchases a new car or a new house, he or she wants to show it off to everyone, which now opens you up to the people interested in purchasing one as well. If the people in their network see your customer is elated with the service received, the probability he or she will recommend you is quite high.

The goal is to stand out to your customers. You don't want to be just another salesperson; you want to be THEIR salesperson. When asked where they purchased the product and from whom, you want them to say, "I bought it from my car/house guy Bob."

Due to this unspoken rule, you want to always be prospecting. Make sure EVERYONE knows what you're selling. Everywhere I went in Orlando, I made sure I carried my business cards and made sure everyone knew what I did and where I did it because when you make friends outside of the environment and leave a lasting impression, when it comes time for them to require your product, they're going to come to you!

It was a dark and rainy night in Orlando and I lived about 30 seconds away from a Kangaroo gas station. I just got home after a night out and it was late; everywhere else was closed and I needed to buy some bottles of water. I hopped in my car and drove to the gas station, still dressed from being out, and grabbed my waters. I ended up striking up a conversation with the cashier; I asked her how her day was and she told me it was a bit rough. I asked her why and stood there listening to her tell me about her day, building a rapport with her until she asked me how my day was.

I told her I had an awesome day at work and had just came back from celebrating. I told her exactly what I did for a living and why I was the best at it. Then handed her my business card and explained if she or anyone she knows ever needs a car and wants to avoid all of typical salesman gimmicks to come and see me. She thanked me and I left. Four days later she was the first customer at the door of my dealership and was asking for me. I was so excited because that was a free lead I made just from being myself and letting people know what I do. Even though she could not purchase the car due to credit, I still showed her an outstanding level of customer service and

her son returned the next day to purchase a car as well as one of her friends. Keep in mind, I never asked her for anyone else once the sale didn't go through, but my superior customer service enabled her to decide to recommend me to others.

Always be prospecting and getting your name out there, at the salon or barber, the Laundromat, the bagel store, everywhere! Word of mouth is always the most powerful form of advertising. You never know whom you're connecting with and what they need or when they need it.

Write down your major takeaways!

"Everyday in every way, I am getting better and better!"

Chapter 5: Maximize Daily

Little do you know, but your day-to-day happenings have a huge impact on your sales. The way you treat your day will reflect on the way you treat people and the number of sales. Think about, if your whole day is disordered and you're not giving your all, what makes you think you can give your all in your sales? Leave no stone unturned and tackle every single day as if it was a customer you're working on selling. You can't climb the ladder of success with your hands in your pockets, so do not cripple yourself by dragging out unnecessary baggage into your sales.

Activate your morning and charge up for the day. When people meet you they want to meet the you that's on top of the world and on your "A" game! For me, every morning starts by charging myself up by re-reading my goals for the day, week, month, and year to align myself with my WHY. Then I do a few minutes of deep breathing to ground and center myself for the day before walking outside toward my car, looking at the sky, and listing three things I am grateful for. On the 15-minute drive from my house to work, I have a giant smile on my face while I listen to music that amps me up to get myself ready to take control of my day. I also imagine the day going exactly how I want it to go, visualizing all of the sales coming my way. So every time I walked through the door, I was READY to work and be the BEST.

Of course I'm not perfect; there were some days I did not do this and would just drive in silence on my way to work, but that's okay! We're human! But as soon as I walked through the doors of my showroom, I immediately dropped everything internal and came in with the mindset to only work. I did not care about anything else going on outside of my life except for my work. I needed to bring all of my focus to work and to my customers.

You're selling yourself short if you're not bringing your "A" game to the table every single day. When people approach you or when you approach them, they can easily feel when your head is not in the game and you're not giving them your full presence, which will make them less inclined to give more to you. The workplace is where it's just you and your work. Remember, where focus goes, energy flows. So when you bring all of your focus to your work where do you think all of that energy is going to go? You'll literally be creating energy from scratch.

I fully believe the reason I was so good was I understood sales. I believe selling is healing and a salesperson is solving a deep problem whenever interacting with a customer. A customer comes in with a problem, maybe something missing in his or her life, and the salesperson is the gateway to what they need, to solving the problem.

With a belief like that I am able to give my all to this person because I truly believe I am healing them. Not only is it healing, but selling is also a transference of energy. People do not care about what you're selling most of the time — they buy you and all of your emotions, states of being, and feelings!

I knew when I got my job I was not selling cars, but rather I was selling myself and I made a commitment to become the best healer around. I told myself while everyone was out selling cars, I was selling myself, which is how I'll rise to the top — and I did.

The key to this chapter is to increase your energy output so people want to be around you and people want to buy *you*. They want to buy how you're making them feel! They want to buy the emotional states you're putting them through. Before any customer interaction, you must activate yourself. Do something that makes you feel powerful and confident. Before I would ever work with any customer I would clap my hands and mentally say, "LET'S GO!" and my body, mind, and spirit immediately knew it was game time; it was time to serve this soul.

Imagine how powerful this would be once you start implementing it in your day-to-day routine. I want you to take time and reflect on some of the sales you have lost in the past. Have you lost them because of the way you were acting? Or maybe you were having a really bad day and the customer perceived your bad energy. Even if it's just for that interaction when you activate yourself for the sale, your sales will skyrocket because you're making yourself very presentable, approachable, and friendly.

I have used this technique with every single person I have ever sold something to, including before I got into professional sales and it has worked.

On my third day at my dealership I was shadowing a superior salesperson. The dealership was becoming overcrowded and with an insufficient supply of salespeople, I was put on the floor. I approached a gentleman, introduced myself to him, and told him I was new but I would do my best to treat him exactly how he wanted to be treated. I began to explain how everything worked in our dealership and he was surprised how laid back I was being. We began talking about life and I expressed this would be the first car I ever sold. He looked at me and laughed exclaiming this would be the first car he ever bought! I told him we would learn together and the sale closed with two extremely happy people. He was so happy after he bought the car he left four rave reviews on multiple websites and even told his best friend to purchase a car from me the next day.

My dealership paid based on volume of sales and customer service reviews. I remember when I first heard I could get paid for delivering outstanding customer service I had a huge grin on because I knew the secret to sales.

When I started, the minimum reviews you needed a month was 10 in order to be able eligible for monthly bonuses. My first month I had 26 reviews; my second month increased to 33. The CEO of the company heard of my chart-breaking reviews and changed the review policy. The following month I had 42 reviews and he changed it again. He changed it every month for the 7 months I was there and I left setting the company record of 80 reviews for a month.

I didn't even care about the volume of cars I was selling, but more about how I could get people to buy my positive energy and be a master at selling myself. This not only brought me to the top of the review charts out of 120 employees, but also to the top in car sales.

Write down your major takeaways!

"In order for us to truly grow we must take full reasonability of what happens in our lives."

Chapter 6: Effectively Blaming

This is one of the most valuable lessons I learned in my life and I have applied it to every aspect of it — my relationships, my sales, and my daily life. This one thing not only increased my sales, but also allowed me to grow significantly whenever a challenge or problem presented itself in front of me.

In sales, when we lose a sale we can't just overlook it. We need to investigate it and ask why because there's a gem waiting for us to collect it and if we keep overlooking it we'll miss that growing opportunity.

I had to ask myself why I lost the sale and what lesson I can learn from it. That is when I realized it was my fault. Now that I was asking myself a more empowering question, my brain started to seek a more empowering answer. I began to reflect and started to see little loopholes that were missed. Now that I was taking full responsibility for what happened, I developed one of the greatest lessons of my life.

When we take full responsibility for the things that happen around us and we don't blame others, we can absorb the lesson a lot more. Our brain will seek out the answers for how we can improve for next time. We can improve upon the one thing we either didn't do or maybe did too much that cost us the sale or maybe it was the relationship that we need to put more effort into.

Typically, in life when we have an expectation and it does not go our way or our expectation is not met, we are often met with disappointment. That disappointment begins the blame game in which we start to blame everyone around us, but ourselves, the one person that will benefit the most from the lesson.

Take the time to look back in your life and your lost sales in which you blamed the customer and ask yourself the questions below. Every time you lose a sale or anytime you're looking back at your sale quota, use these questions as a guideline to help you decode it.

- *Where did it go wrong?*
- *How could I have met his/her needs better?*
- *What is the one thing I can learn about myself from this interaction?*
- *What can I bring from this interaction into my next one?*

Now, you won't be able to close every single sale; sometimes it might even take a customer a couple of years to buy from you. Nevertheless, this questioning process will allow you to decode and constantly refine your process along the way. There's always going to be he next level for you to reach. There's no such thing as a perfect process, but there is the art of perfecting along the way.

There's a sales term I would hear on a continual basis, even before I began sales. As unsuitable as it may seem, it's a true testament to many customers: buyers are liars.

"Buyers are liars," suggests customers never mean what they say. One second they say they were just looking and the next they're handing you a down-payment though telling they had no intention of buying your product today.

They come in saying they want a very specific product and then see something else for which their heart immediately goes out to and they forget everything they said about the first one.

One of the biggest lies in the entire sales industry is when a customer states, "Just looking." There's a reason they came to check out your inventory and it is not because they're "just looking," but because THEY'RE INTERESTED! They came inside of your establishment to look at your products; therefore, can be closed on!

If a customer tells you they're "just looking" and you let him/her walk away, you're leaving a lot of money on the table. If you don't close the sale, someone else will. They're looking for the one person that stands out and they can connect to and earn their trust.

Keep in mind you are also a customer and/or buyer and can be guilty of doing this as well. If you can take a step back and look at the way you shop, you can learn a lot about other customers.

While writing this book, I moved to a new city. The first thing I did was create a list of all the gyms in my local area so I could spend the next week checking each one out to see how each one treated me, if they had the equipment I was looking for, and which ultimately met my standards. At the first gym, as soon as I walked in I was greeted by an extremely friendly girl that gave me a tour of the gym. As soon as the tour started, we were laughing, making great conversation, and she was asking me what I was looking for before showing me everything (remember, you want meet the customer's needs). After our tour she showed me the prices and I thanked her explaining I was looking at multiple gyms. During my whole workout, I couldn't stop imagining myself working out at any other gym. This gym had a friendly staff and what I needed; I immediately signed up and have not regretted the decision since.

I truly believe if the salesperson did not engage me the way she did I would have taken my business elsewhere.

She didn't employ hard closing tactics, just got to know me as a person, and even though I told her I was just looking she pursed it in a non-aggressive way.

Always stick to your sales process and serve the customer, even if he/she is "just looking" because usually the ones not interested at the moment are the ones that buy that day.

Times have changed and people don't like to be forced or handled. Show them you care and you're there for them. People always buy from people they trust. If you lose a sale, it's *your* fault. Now that you're fully aware of it, look back because this will help skyrocket your personal growth and help you become a master of your craft.

At the end of every day reexamine your day. Look at all your sales and all you lost that day. Ask yourself questions and possibly keep track of it to measure your progress.

Look at your sales and ask yourself:

- *How could I have done this better?*
- *What did I do that was spectacular?*
- *Did I almost do something to lose the sale? If so, how did I recover?*

If you can't figure out why you lost a sale, you can be a bit daring and actually call up your customer and ask them what you could've improved on. No one will give you a more clear answer than the customer. Sometimes the only thing that separates a sale from a loss is something as small as losing the opportunity to make the customer smile.

Your goal is to create a sales timeline for yourself. Create a process that takes your customer and leads him/her along the line from start to finish. Once you have your clear process set out, you can easily find the holes and ways to perfect it along the way.

My sales process was to greet the customer, show him/her how to find a car in our system, point to the lot where he/she could find a car. Next, I told the customer to re-enter the showroom and find me in order for me to pull the car up for them, do a walk around, and through a series of questions I would elicit whether they were serious so we could go on a test drive. After the drive, we would go back into the showroom and begin the paperwork.

Sometimes the customer would come and immediately tell me he/she wanted to drive a specific car and I would agree and use my communication skills to veer him/her back on my proven process. One of my general managers said it best, in a very comedic way. He said, "Imagine your sales process is like a date. You don't just tell your date everything about yourself in the first hour! You need to slowly work it. Slowly give more and more information about yourself as you continue so you can keep her interested and wanting more. Never move too quick!"

Write down your major takeaways!

_____

"Refuse to be ordinary!"

Chapter 7: X-Factor

This book is about making you the X-factor sales professional. Getting you from the ordinary salesperson to YOUR customer's salesperson. You want the customer to introduce you as "he/she is my (insert product) sales professional."

A lot of people tend to just wait for leads to come their way and when you take an approach like that you will have some success, but not enough to make you crush it in your sales game. You are not going to wait for leads anymore; you are going to create them. Referrals come to those who earn them. I hate to say it, but don't go around expecting people to just give you referrals. You need to earn them through exceptional customer service.

In this chapter, I'm going to teach you something only the best of the best use. This is on a whole other level of adding value you won't really hear about.

One of the techniques I used to get more referrals was to literally ask. There's a very famous quote that says, "Ask and ye shall receive." I created a sheet with 3 form on it to fill out for contact information from three referrals. I would give this form to customers I connected with extremely well. I've made enough despotism into the customer bank that when I wanted to withdraw from it, I had enough money.

Another strategy is to get in front of as many people as you can and into their homes through thank you cards. Imagine every time you go and check your mail all you get are a bunch of bills and grocery store ads. It's not very exciting to check the mail unless you have a package coming. Now think back to a time when you went to go check the mail and there was a letter FOR YOU! You get a little excited and relieved it's not another bill! The fact someone had the time and energy to send you something in the mail shows they were thinking of you. Why not make your customer feel special? I have a friend who is a master appreciator and his sales are always through the roof because he knows how to achieve greatness through gratitude by being a master at sending thank you notes to his customers.

For those of you whom do not know, there is a man, Joe Girard, whom holds the Guinness Book of World Records for most cars ever sold (13,001). He attributes most of this to the same technique After every single interaction with a customer, purchased or not, he would send them a customized card regarding the encounter. Not only is this an effective strategy, but you're also getting in their homes. I don't know about you, but whenever I get a greeting card I usually keep them around for a bit and look at them from time to time, especially when they have a really nice message!

Now I know you're thinking—I want leads and this is a perfect way to ask for leads! It's not. The point of this is not to send the card and put a message in saying, "It was such a pleasure meeting you! The best compliment is a referral" because that's the first step OUT of their house!

We want to add value and show we care. Keep track of every single one of your customers and specific information you have gathered such as how many kids they have, what they love about life, what product they bought or looked at, and even when their birthdays are.

You have all of that information so when you connect with them again you already know about them. That's going to make the customer feel special and send you more business, especially if you make their friends and family feel as amazing as you're making them feel. On your customers' birthdays send them cards just wishing them a happy birthday or send cards throughout the holidays. What you're doing is keeping in contact and staying in proximity with him/her through frequency; when someone asks him/her about buying a car, the customer will immediately refer you because you're doing what no else is doing and staying in contact.

You may be thinking, "Omid, I don't want to spend all of this money on postage and cards!" Nonetheless, if you really think about it, one referral could make you a sale that would provide enough commission to cover all of your costs and give you much more money in the bank.

Treat your sales as your own business and as if you're the CEO. This is just a business investment and investments have an ROI and you're using this ROI to net you more sales, which will ultimately increase your numbers and help you earn more money and referrals. Remember this is business; you're going to need to spend some money to make money.

Another thing Joe Girard did that brought him a lot of referrals was paying the person who gave him a referral and he made sure everyone around him knew it. Every single person he sold to or even those that did not buy he would offer $25 for every person they recommended to him. Do you see the key? Yet even the man that sold the most cars in the world knew he could not close every sale and still offered to pay just for the referral. It's a win-win situation for everyone involved.

Average people do what's required; successful people go above and beyond what's expected. If you do what you've always done, you'll get what you've always gotten. It's time to shake it up a bit and try out new strategies. If you're going to want to be the best you're going to have to change everything up!

Write down your major takeaways!

_____

"Whether you think you can, or can't - you're right"

Chapter 8: Full Circle

Whenever I start something, I like to tie it all together in the end, bringing it into a full circle and hitting all of the most important points again.

There is not the final chapter; this doesn't end. This is something you take with your into your daily routine because it not only helps bring you more referrals, make you more money, and increase sales, but it also helps enrich your relationships throughout your entire life.

My goal writing this book was to give you tools to use in your professional and personal life. All of these skills, strategies, and tips correlate with the real world and you'd be surprised how each of these areas helps each other.

With this chapter I want to give you some of my last tips and techniques to propel you once you are ready to begin to apply what you've learned. In terms of the 80/20 system, business is 80% psychology and 20% production. If you plan on running your sales like your own business, then you have to master every part of it.

I want to focus a great deal on the psychology of humans and the correlation to sales. The great Henry Ford said, "Whether you think you can or can't, you're right." Take this phrase in and really dissect the message it's trying to portray. The only person standing in your way is you. All of the battles you face in this world are just you vs. yourself. You may think you're facing an external opponent, but in reality it's just a reflection of you projecting into the outside world. Some of us think the opponent is our customer. That's why I stress the fact that you need to take a step back and analyze the situation.

I do not believe we can sell every customer, but there is something…ONE THING…that can always change a lost deal into a closed deal. Through accepting that every lost deal is our fault, we are more open to the learning possibilities to close the next customer. It will all come down to you and how you handle everything and use this in your life. When there is no outside enemy to hurt you become friends with who you are within.

I know there is no such thing as perfection, but I do believe in progress and perfecting along the way. I don't think we'll ever have a perfect relationship with ourselves as we are humans and we do have positive and negative emotions. Nevertheless, if we create an environment in which the positives outweigh the negatives, our relationships will be closer to perfect than not. Once you can become a master of your emotions, you will see how it begins to reflect in your day and especially in your sales.

It's more than the way you treat your customers; it is also how you treat yourself because you are your ultimate customer. If you can't sell yourself there's no way you can sell someone else.

Here are some great ways to master more of you.

- *Meditation*
- *Exercise*
- *Positive incantations*
- *"I am…" statements*
- *Your environment*
- *Awareness*
- *FUN*

Meditation: meditation is something that excels everything. It's the perfect tool to becoming a better you. It helps bring peace into your life and release a lot of unnecessary stress you don't need. Image your mind is like the ocean; on a day-to-day basis it's usually rocking as if going through a massive storm. What meditation does is help to calm those waters to a stillness in which one pebble can fall and create a massive ripple throughout.

Meditation allows you to access a different part of your mind. It also helps you find more answers.. You can do guided meditations or close your eyes and put some classical music on and just breathe deeply allowing yourself to visualize what you want in life. Meditation does not have to be a huge part of your day either. You can do it for as short as 10 minutes a day. Either way I invite you to be open-minded and give this a shot. Even if you have never done it before. If you go to the website www.alwaysbeclosingbook.com/meditation, I give you a free list of all the meditations I recommend doing.

Exercise: THIS IS HUGE! Your body is the only vehicle you have to live in and your only home. It's what's going to give you the energy in order to work, create, meet more people, and close more sales. If you don't have energy you can't do anything.

I know you've had days in your life where your energy level is extremely low and you can't produce anything.

Now I'm not saying to commit your whole life to becoming an exercise junkie, but just move your body! What you don't use, you lose. Go out and walk or take a yoga class or just stretch at home. Health is our greatest wealth and if we're helping our body move it will grant us more energy so you don't need to rely on caffeine in order to operate. I used to work with people that couldn't operate without an energy drink. We live in the age of information where everything and anything we want to learn is all at our fingertips. I encourage you to go and do some research on ways you can get your body moving, ways you can engage some of your muscles and open up those tight muscles for more oxygen to flow.

Just like in life, it's not possible for us to spot reduction. In the bodybuilding world, spot reducing is a term that means you only focus on losing fat in one area of your body. That's impossible because your body has to enter a fat burning mode and it burns fat THROUGHOUT. In life, you have multiple areas, yet you tend to focus on one. Include ALL of the areas in your life and body and GET MOVING!

Positive incantations: I'm sure you can agree we are constantly speaking to ourselves. Unfortunately, most of the time it's negative self talk…so why not set the rules for us to win? If we're going to talk to ourselves we might as well flood our inner voice with nothing but positive words and phrases. Train your mind to believe and create whatever you want.

Incantations are affirmations with more power, emotion, and reaction attached to it. An affirmation is a way to get a phrase to remain in your mind through repetition such as, "I'm happy, I'm happy, I'm happy," until you choose to believe it. When you restate an incantation, speak it, embody it, and bring everything you have to what you are saying.

Get creative with them — rhyme them if you can, fill them with words that will excite you every time you speak it. The intention of this is to absolutely charge you up every time you embody it. Whenever this incantation leaves your lips, it's as if you're putting your whole soul into it.

Here's an example of one of my earlier incantations:

"At last the past is past. I, Omid Kazravan, am fueled for life. I have an intense burning passion for sharing my outstanding charisma with the people around me. I have a fire within that melts away all the limitations! I am extremely ecstatic for my life because I am a motivational beast that cannot be tamed. Everything I do I turn on BEAST mode and give it my all. I am a master strategist ready to put my wondrous creativity to work. The universe's wealth is circulating in my life, flowing to me in avalanches of abundance. All my needs, desires, and goals are met instantaneously by infinite intelligence. I am a vibrant, active, alive, dynamic, and energetic soul. I am extremely grateful for my health and my well being. I am SUCCESS."

Now, it does not need to be as long as mine, but rather shorter and to the point. It can be a sentence if you want. One of my favorite short incantations is: "ALL I NEED IS WITHIN ME NOW."It's straight and to the point and gets my absolutely enthusiastic when I say it. Remember, it does not have to stick with you for the rest of your life! It's okay to constantly change it as you mature.

Here's one of legendary speaker Tony Robbins' incantations he states before every client or an audience:

"I now command my subconscious mind to direct me in helping as many people as possible today to better their lives, by giving me the strength, the emotion, the persuasion, the humor, the brevity, whatever it takes to show these people and get these people to change their life now!"

Go ahead and be creative with yours! Feel free to check the thesaurus for synonyms to really bring excitement and a smile to your face.

"I am..." statements: These are the same concept as incantations. We are not just saying out I ams, but we are physically embodying them and speaking them aloud into the world. It's best if you PUT EMOTION INTO IT! Convince yourself it's going to change your life; you must believe in it fully in order for it to take effect. Remember, you are rewiring years and years of thought patterns into something to truly serve us on a higher level. Make sure your I ams and your incantations are aligned with your beliefs as well.

These are my I AMS I say on a daily basis:

- I am *Loved*
- I am *Creative*
- I am *Guided*
- I am *Centered*
- I am *Grounded*
- I am *Passionate*
- I am *Grateful*
- I am *Charismatic*

I repeat these when I am driving or going for a walk or run. If I'm in the car, I will blast my music and then proceed to yell all of these at the top of my lungs and get my whole body involved including my facial expressions and create the intensity and purpose to WILL change in my life.

Do you want to be more of a patient person? Maybe you want to be more creative and don't feel like you are? Allow your imagination to go wild and don't limit it. Anything is possible. Make sure your I ams are in a positive tense. Our brains cannot register the negative tense so if you're saying, "I am not ____," your brain will register that you are that! This is all part of the process of creating our life by design and remember successful people do what failures don't. Go ahead and create yours, but remember to write it down.

Your environment: You are the people you surround yourself with. I remember when I was working at my dealership it became my second home. I would spend anywhere from 60-85 hours a week there so these were the people I would constantly surround myself with.

I remember many coworkers would complain a lot and do nothing but put negative energy out into the world.

Do you see how these type of people can bring you down if you allow it to? That's the power of negative people. I remember catching myself acquiring some of their habits and repeating their negative comments. I had to catch myself and remind myself who I was.

Don't join the negative club; instead use that time to create opportunities for yourself in your sales. While they're complaining, go make a sale because what you put out will ultimately come back to you so if you're doing nothing but leaving negative energy in the room, that's what you'll receive. Instead, generate a positive environment that will encourage your growth whether it's in your workplace or outside. Regardless of how much change we want, if our environment is extremely toxic chances are we will either never make the change or it will be extremely hard.

Awareness: The first step to change is to be aware there is something that needs to be changed. Be aware of your weaknesses, of what's going on around you, what's causing you to do something, or why you're reacting the way you are.

Become a master of analyzing yourself. Always ask yourself WHY you do something because once you can figure out yourself you'll be know what makes you tick and you'll be able to replicate it.

If you feel a certain emotion, take a step back and ask yourself why you're feeling that way. What would you need to do in that moment to stop or start to feel that emotion? If you can't think of something, just pretend you know the answer and it will magically come to you!!

FUN: Finally, this is what it should be about — fun. If you're not having fun, something is wrong. You need to have fun in what you do because your fun will leak out and become contagious; people will want to be around you because you're just a genuinely fun person.

Always ask yourself how can you make this task more fun. Be a creative, like a hungry explorer always looking for opportunities! Something I always disliked was putting air in my customers' tires. However, I created a game out of it; I decided to race myself per tire and create a personal time. Doing that excited me to pump air because it was an activity that did not seem dull anymore.

When things become dull you tend to not want to give your best anymore. If it's not fun, it's not worth the hassle. If you're not having fun you either need to figure out why you're not having fun or change your career. Life is too short not to be having fun.

Write down your major takeaways!

_____

"There is no such thing as failure, only results."

Chapter 9: Conclusion

You are needed in this world, in this society. Salespeople make the wheel go round because if we don't help remove the goods off of the shelves, the whole system stops running. We are the engines to the whole operation.

Once you adopt this belief you'll begin to feel a lot more fulfilled because you're immediately doing something far greater than yourself. Imagine a food chain—even if one component of the food chain was missing, it would create a massive ripple and ultimately disrupt the whole ecosystem.

Next time you interact with a customer remember he or she is not just purchasing the product, but you as well. If you leave a negative impression, you are also leaving a negative impression on every single person the customer spoke to. Now let's look at the other side of the coin.

Think back to a time when someone left a lasting impression on you. Once you have that person in mind, think about how you felt and also think about whom you told about your experience. That person just got a lot of free exposure just by being a great salesperson.

Your customer appreciates a salesperson that will go the extra mile and give an honest interpretation. This helps to construct your rapport and relationship between you and your customer. As a salesperson the ultimate goal is closing a sale; by serving your customer and initiating an honest, trustworthy affinity, YOU WILL CLOSE THE SALE!

Its time for you to take on everything that you have learned and go and apply it. All it takes for you to double or triple your income and sales is just ONE thing. There is no reason for you to overload yourself with information if in the end you don't use anything you've learned.

Thank you so much for taking the time to read this book. I feel very blessed and grateful that I have had the opportunity to get share my learnings with you and benefit the quality of your life. I hope I get to meet you at some point!

Acknowledgements

Out of the whole book this chapter is probably the hardest one to write. There are so many people that I have met throughout my life that have added immense amounts of value to my life.

Relationships are the true currency of life. The more quality you have in your relationships the more fulfilled you will feel. I am where I am today because of the influence the people I have surrounded myself with have had on me.

"Show me your friends, and I will show you who you are." This quote always sticks out to me because you are the total of the five people you hang around the most. I feel very honored to have been able to surround myself with nothing but true greatness.

It would take me forever to sit here and thank everyone. I'm going to start off with the people that have had the most impact first.

Mom: My beautiful mother, I love you dearly. It is because of you that I am where I am today. Raising me, as a single mother, was no easy task but you made countless sacrifices and pulled through. You used to work three jobs just to pay the bills, and feed the two of us when I was younger. My whole life you instilled the belief that I could do, be and create anything I wanted to; as long as I had a vision for it and worked my ass off. You were my Tony Robbins before I even knew him. You are the greatest saleswoman I have ever met in my life, you are the embodiment of unconditional love, a true hustler and the greatest mother to walk this planet.

Nick: My brother from another. At the time of me writing this book, we are going on 12 years of friendship. You have always been there when I needed it, and you always know exactly what to say and when to say it. During the lowest points of my life, I always knew that you would show up 100% when I called; and be the best mate a dude could ask for. I do not know where I would be on my journey if I did not have you by my side. You are always keeping me humble and always catching things that I do that I never see myself. I love you. Thank you.

Juan: You are like my older brother, always looking out for me and always keeping me out of trouble. Anytime I come to you with a reason as to why I can not do something, you immediately shatter that BS story I have playing in my head. You are one of the greatest inspirations in my life and every day I am honored that I get to call you a brother. You have always held me to my highest standard since the day I met you. I always know I can count on you whenever I need to discuss a new idea, relationship, or new business venture. It is because of you and Luis that I am taking action towards anything to do with my passion. I love you. Thank you.

Luis: THIS GUY! You are the definition of hustle. You are the last person I ever want to let down. I know that if I tell you I am going to do something then that means I need to do it. If I do not, there will be an endless amount of roasting. You have shown me the ropes to so many things regarding our industry. You are not only my mentor but also my other brother. Anytime I'm about to do something I always ask myself "What would Luis do?" You have such a deep care for those around you, and it shows in your day to day actions as well as how you interact with everyone. Despite how super busy you are, you set aside time to talk with me anytime I call. That means the world. If I would never have met you, I would be miles behind. I love you. Thank you.

Kazravan Family: Thank you so much for helping my mother to raise me. You have instilled so much love in my life just because you all exude love. Thank you for helping me create beautiful memories, being there when I needed it the most, and showing endless amounts of support and appreciation. I love you, thank you.

"Work so hard that your idols become your friends."

Tony Robbins: I have yet to meet you but for the past 10 years you have been the greatest source of inspiration and motivation in my life. Since the age of 12 I have been listening and applying everything you have been teaching. I have been raised off of your teachings. Anytime I feel that times are getting rough and want to throw the towel in I always think back to your story of your upbringing. If you were to quit when you were faced with all those hardships then my life would have never been impacted and I would not be here, nor would I have met the amazing people in my life. Once I connect with that I know that I need to keep doing this for those similar to myself out in the world. Keep doing what you're doing and I can't wait for the day I get to share a stage with you and call you one of my dear friends. I love you, Thank you.

Friends: Sergio, Adriana, Lola, Michael Savage, Chuck, Felix, Mina Shah if I missed your name you all know exactly who you are. Thank you for being a part of my life and making my life worth living. I wouldn't trade the memories we have created for anything. Our roots run very deep and all I want do is share my success with all of you.

Thank you all for your support and all the laughs we've shared together. I love you, Thank you.

You: Thank you most of all. You are the reason I wake up to work, and the reason I spend hours creating content. I would not be doing this if you weren't here. Anytime I am creating something I know that there are those people out there that need to hear what I have to say. Thank you for being you. My vision is to impact a million people (You included) and to show people how to increase the quality of their lives.

Your Gift

Because you took action to invest in yourself.
I am giving you FREE access to a few bonuses

Visit this site www.Alwaysbempire.com
NOW to get exclusive access to 6 different sales
tracking worksheets that you can use and apply
in your business TODAY! The best part about
this offer is that it is completely free. No
gimmicks.

TONY ROBBINS SAYS "What doesn't get
measured doesn't managed"

This is my gift to you to elevate your sales
game

I Need your help…
Can you please review this book?

If you enjoyed this book and/or this book added value to your life can you please go and take a quick second to review it? Your review will go a very long way and allow this book to reach more people. Let's do this as a team!

Thank you again for downloading this book!

You can leave a review for this book on Amazon by going to where you purchased this book and click on "leave a review".

Thank you and good luck!

Made in the USA
San Bernardino, CA
16 February 2020